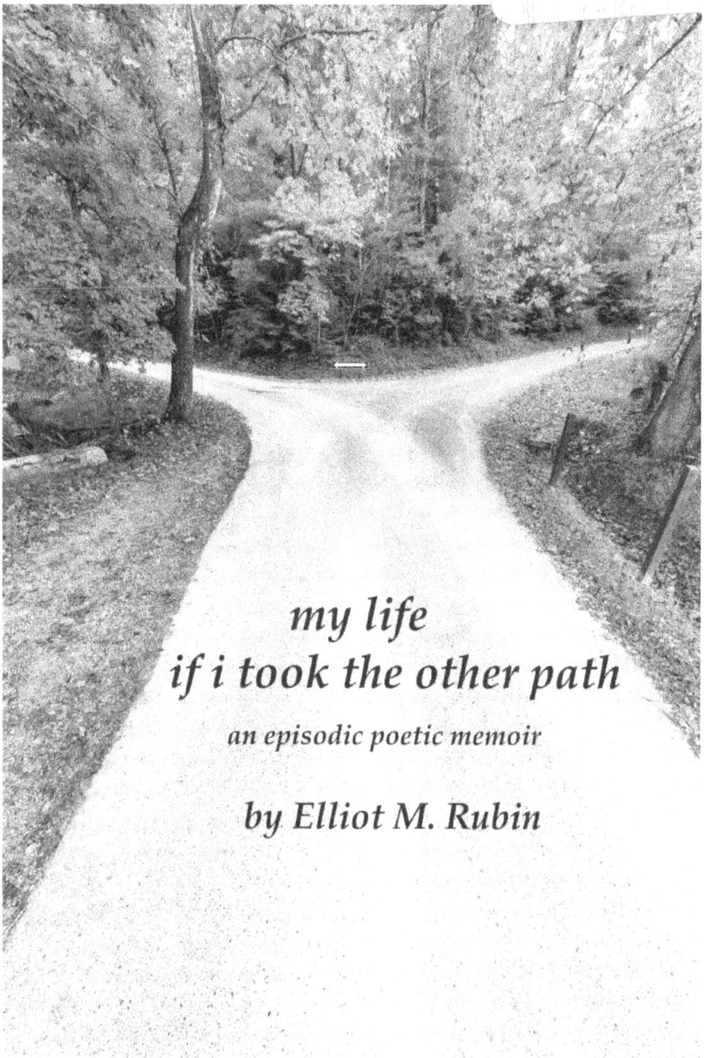

# my life
# if i took the other path
### an episodic poetic memoir

## by Elliot M. Rubin

my life

if i took the other path©

an episodic poetic memoir

by Elliot M. Rubin

Copyright March 2019

Library of Congress

ISBN13 - 978-0-9981796-7-4

ISBN 10 - 0-9981796-7-1

No part of this book may be reproduced in any form whatsoever without the prior, express written consent of the author.

This book is fiction, and all names, people, places, and happenings are from the author's imagination and are used fictionally.

Any resemblance to any living or dead persons, and/or businesses, locations and/or events is coincidental in its entirety.

All rights reserved

## Prologue

This fictional memoir in poetry is an imagined account of what I thought my life could have been if I decided to take a different path, rather than the one I did.

As a young boy I wanted to be a musician and transfer from one of the best academic high schools in New York to Music and Arts; but my father, an accountant, talked me out of it.

I ended up successful in business but always thought what could have been. This book tells the story if I chose the other path.

## Dedication

To others who carried creative thoughts and dreams in their minds, but never acted on them until later in life.

## Table of Contents

my other self ......................................................... 6

awakening ............................................................ 7

Vanessa ................................................................. 9

O'Bryan's bar ...................................................... 11

Utica, New York ................................................. 13

goodbye Vanessa ................................................ 17

tomorrow ............................................................. 19

from the beginning ............................................ 21

Iowa ..................................................................... 24

Cheyenne Wyoming ........................................... 29

Salt Lake City ..................................................... 33

San Francisco ..................................................... 34

west coast living ................................................. 38

Mexico ................................................................. 43

domestication ..................................................... 46

the east coast tour .............................................. 47

the last trip ......................................................... 49

family .................................................................. 51

the call ................................................................ 53

going home ......................................................... 54

**my other self**

sometimes
i wonder,
dream,
imagine,
what my life would be
if i lived it as a
hippie,
free spirit,
a creative bohemian
in a three-piece-suited world

how would i do it differently?

marriage,
family,
lifestyle,
career,
what would i consider success?

where would i live?
city, suburb, rural,
somewhere remote?
mountains,
forest, desert,
or a California commune?

free love,
drugs,
multiple partners,
living on the wild side?

don't we all, secretly, think what if?

**awakening**

the sun burst through
never washed windows
waking me
from a deep,
drunken sleep

turning my head
to bury it in my pillow,
i felt her stale morning breath
envelope my face,
joining the morning's
bright rays
flushing me
from my bed,
escaping to the toilet
to return
last night's indulgence
of cheap whiskey;
where it probably belongs

i know where i am
but who is she?
i don't know her,
or recognize the naked
body lying on my bed

she's not bad looking.
kind of young though
to be with an old fart
like myself,
i hope i had a good time;
guess i'll find out soon enough

her eyes start to open-

looking at my corpulent
naked torso,
a sly smile peeks out
on pink
supple lips,
while her hand
motions me to rejoin her
on the bed

good lord,
she must be a third
of my age;
glad she didn't kill
me last night-
i don't recall hearing
the coal miner's
caged canary sing,
so everything
must have been okay;
i wonder who she is?

just another cheap, barfly hooker
looking for an old trick to fleece?
to make me want to keep her,
to feel young,
wanted,
useful again;
only to find her leave one day
breaking my heart?

whiskey doesn't leave you
until you have too much-
just like this young piece of ass will
do one day; when she has too much
of me, like the others did

## Vanessa

i don't even know her name

she motions for me to rejoin her
on my bed, so i slide under the blanket-
we snuggle and shove our tongues
in each other's mouth;
we fool around till exhausted,
then asks me for my name

as we talk i kind of remember
her coming into O'Bryan's last night,
sitting next to me in the booth-
that's about it before i blacked out

now we are entangled in each other's arms

stroking her hair,
looking closely at her appearance,
the long,
bleached blond tresses
with pink highlights
have black roots,
the youthful face
carries a river of lines
hidden below caked on makeup-
up-close the toothy smile shows a few gaps,
and the track marks on her arms
tell me her life story

if only she were a princess
filled with goodness,
sent here to be my lifetime
companion;
i would like a fairy tale ending

trouble is, i know when her next fix
comes due she will disappear
in the filthy bowels of Utica;
like the pumpkin at midnight,
except i'll have no glass shoe
to hold in my hands,
just fond memories
of one great morning
of mind-blowing sex
in a shit hole town,
in the god damn middle
of fucking nowhere

**O'Bryan's bar**

this small, one-traffic-light town
hidden
in the mountains of upstate New York,
near Old Forge,
has three bars,
one post office,
and a general store
where i buy most of my needs
when i need them

a lot of folks up here
live in trailers,
some have cabins buried deep in the woods,
a few even rent rooms
in the handful of single-family homes
scattered around town

i came here years ago,
settled down in a few back rooms
of the town's main whore;
we live separate lives, and
don't get together much
in the way lonely folks here do

after i finish writing for the day
i pull a Hemingway-
i visit my favorite bar,
stay until dinnertime
or passing out
in a rear corner booth till closing

once i was sitting at the bar nursing
a twelve-year-old triple distilled,
smooth, single malt scotch,

when two young guys
come strutting in the door

one of them pulls a gun on O'Bryan
demanding cash from the register,
while his buddy stood at the entrance.
i took a sip of my drink, ignoring him,
looking straight ahead into the mirror
at the back of the bar,
while O'Bryan reaches down
between the bottles,
pulling out his Glock,
putting three holes in the young man's chest

his blood-splattered
all over the floor,
the bar,
my right arm,
but thankfully
didn't go into my whiskey
cause my hand was over it;
picking up my glass
i stepped over the body
heading for my booth
to finish out the evening
in my solitude,
till the bar closed

the sad part happened
much later in the evening,
a state trooper
came to investigate;
he discovered the guy died for nothing -
he used a fake replica gun

## Utica, New York

it sucks to be old and horny,
forces a man to do stupid things.
against my better judgment
i give her forty dollars,
then drove to Utica
for the girl to meet a drug dealer
in my suicidal fifteen-year-old
piece of crap Buick,
with the rear bumper hanging on
by a single bolt,
dragging the muffler
under the car, while
driving along the road
sending sparks upward
toward the gasoline tank

i try to justify my helping her.
my addiction is booze,
hers are opioids-
both in the long run
deadly,
life defeating habits
best not to start with

but this is a reality-
together, we're both run down
companions in misery
who happen to find one another
in this forested,
bucolic area,
overrun with toothless redneck hunters
and backwoods types,
salivating to shoot some living thing
for sport

she directs me
to a desolate area of the city;
i park a few feet from a corner
where a bunch of guys
wearing hoodies are gathered
under a cloud of pungent smoke from weed

i notice a bulge
under the fleece of one of them;
guessing what is in his waistband

i keep the motor running
as Vanessa jumps out
walking toward them
focusing on one individual

the guy recognizes her,
smiling, expecting a payday

their hands extend and touch;
he takes her cash,
she puts something in her pocket,
then turns back to me
heading for the car,
staring straight ahead
expressionless

i must be nuts to get implicated
in a drug transaction like this-
when you're seventy-three
and the girl is twenty-five
an old man
will do things he shouldn't;
foolish things,
dangerous even,
when a decision regarding continued,

unexpected,
great sex is involved

i decide to have a heart-to-heart talk
with her on the way back

told me she is divorced
left an abusive husband
lost custody of her daughter
uses drugs to numb her loss;
her feelings of betrayal by him,
a supposed life partner
devastated her psyche

she later met a guy
who turned out to be a drug dealer,
her dealer-
she ran away
when he started to beat her,
pimping her out;
by sheer chance one night at O'Bryan's
i became her escape route

i notice beads of perspiration
forming on her forehead;
she needs a fix-
so i speed up
on the rural back roads

once we get to my apartment
she runs
in the bathroom
and shoots up

then

silence

no sounds

a few minutes later,
  she quietly
    walks out,
      lays down
        on my bed,
and falls asleep
 entangled,
   yet secure
    in my arms

**goodbye Vanessa**

she sleeps through the night
while i tumble over in my head
how i became so involved
in this screwed up girl's life

two days ago
i didn't even know her,
now i'm financing
her drug habit-
somehow,
this has to stop.

i can't do this;
i'll miss her,
i'll miss the sex…
i decide she has to leave tomorrow

finally,
holding her warm
naked body
next to mine,
i fall asleep

the next morning
i wake up
to an empty bed,
calling out to her
there is no answer-
the bathroom light is on,
i walk-in
to see her sprawled on the floor,
a needle is hanging
from her forearm

dialing nine one one
a volunteer ambulance unit
is sent to respond;
there are no damn doctors around here,
it is from the next town, up the road,
and takes a while to arrive

the head EMT gives her a shot
of something to counter-act the drug-
the problem
is the unit took a long time to arrive

finally, they place her in the ambulance
then drive away to the local County Hospital

the EMT told me
before he left with her
it is touch and go

i'm not sure Vanessa will make it

**tomorrow**

the next day
as soon as O'Bryan opens
i'm drinking
my Jameson twelve-year-old
single malt scotch,
trying to drown out
my unexpected
yet continuing depression,
the possibility of losing her

a girl i only just met,
a total stranger
until a day ago,
somehow, we played
into each other's desperate needs;
we bonded

after a few sips,
i call the hospital
to find out if she is okay

i inform them i am her father;
if she is alive, they might tell me
something,
anything

they are going to release her tomorrow

relieved,
anxiety abated,
my mind finally relaxes

i'm starting to get tipsy
so i head for the back booth,

my refuge
to drink alone,
feeling miserable
until O'Bryan walks over
to sit down
across from me

he asks
what is going on
since it is too early in the day
for me to show up drinking;
it is not yet noon

i start to tell him my life story

**from the beginning**

in my early school years
i was a dreamer-
imagining different places
and people
while the teacher droned on
in a monotone voice
putting me to sleep,
sprouting words without meaning;
just sounds to my ears
while i was mentally elsewhere

although i never failed a grade promotion
i didn't earn any awards or citations either,
not even for good attendance

although, in sixth grade
i was made the eraser monitor
who went outside
every afternoon to clap
the white chalk out of them,
while breathing
in the powered
cloud of fine dust
clogging my young clear lungs,
only later in life
to regret being chosen

in high school
i learned to play guitar,
was in a few bands-
one day i met
eighteen-year-old Leslie;
tall,
straight blond hair down her back,

high fashion looking,
model-thin as a rail
with a lithe body,
and a pasty white complexion;
who chain-smoked
Parliament cigarettes

one day she led me down a path
of excitement,
alcohol,
drugs,
and sexual debauchery

as a sixteen-year-old boy
who was enamored of her
i didn't want it to end

being an avid reader
it helped with my poetry-
i performed my own songs
from the poems i wrote
then sang them for her

after graduation,
i was accepted to college
as an English major;
Leslie dropped out

she went to San Francisco
to live life

she left me

i was jealous of her,
wishing,
badly desiring if only

i could join in her adventure

nineteen sixty-three was at the beginning
of the hippie era,
California was the place to be-
i didn't have money
or the age
to travel with her
so i hung out
in the East Village in Manhattan;
there i found a few Leslie substitutes
to overcome my sense of loss

my poems were published
in the Village Voice
plus other local underground newspapers

the dingy basement coffee shops
held open mike nights
where i read my stuff-
to my surprise
i developed a following,
young girls,
hippie chicks,
and older
mature women
who sprinkled me
with gifts, i couldn't afford,
usually when they took me home
after a performance

it was great to be seventeen in Manhattan

**Iowa**

when i turned eighteen
i wanted,
i needed,
more satisfaction

words escape me to describe
my wanderlust then, but
i heard California call to me-
or my longing for Leslie;
so i left home

sharing an apartment
in Brooklyn with four guys,
working part-time
menial jobs to survive
as a poet and writer-
an undernourished one,
i saved every penny
i made-
took a Greyhound bus
to San Francisco
to make my fame and fortune;
then hook up with Leslie again,
hopefully

although the west coast
is warmer than New York
the rest of the country in winter
is cold,
snowy,
roads can be too dangerous
to drive on-
the police
do close them down if unsafe

Iowa may be a beautiful state
in less harsh weather, but
it sucks in winter-
police made the bus
pull off the interstate
near Des Moines;
it stopped
at a rundown motel
with a small restaurant attached,
in a two-bit town
where everyone,
including myself,
left the bus

a few of us
walked in to see
if anything was cheap enough to eat-
let alone clean

i had enough cash
to buy some buttered toast-
with the glass of water
the waitress gave me,
i squeezed lemon slices
from a monkey dish,
adding sugar packets
to make a poor mans
somewhat drinkable
homemade lemonade

the waitress stopped
at my table to talk to me,
i guess she is lonely;
we are the only ones left in the place
as the others ate
then went back to the bus,

or took a room
in the fleabag motel

she walked back to the kitchen,
then a few minutes later
brought out a burger and fries
with a soda for me;
i was hungry and thanked her

the snow didn't stop,
the bus was stuck
in a town in the middle of nowhere-
i'm in a dirty window dive,
smudged,
handwritten menu items
taped to the walls
with a middle-aged,
slightly plump waitress
in a soiled red apron
and stringy brown hair
flirting
with the only male in the place

young meat to her,
a warm bed to me…
for the night

we left in her pickup truck,
she drove me to her place

we talked a lot in bed,
i think she was lonely.
asking where i am going,
what i am doing with my life
small talk
meaningless

her boyfriend left her
years ago;
stuck her with two kids
she had with him

one day he decided
he wanted to be free
of obligations-
*birds need to fly,*
*fish have to swim,*
and he is gone;
last she heard
he is in Alaska
working on oil rigs,
abandoning his family-
i felt sorry for her

the next morning
i awoke about six
in a decrepit bedroom
in the middle of a trailer park,
surrounded by fields of snow
as far as i could see

when i walked into her kitchen
she is standing next to the stove
naked,
with floppy, pancake breasts
hanging down her chest

breakfast was already made,
eggs, bacon, and coffee,
plus a sandwich for the bus trip

we had one last fling
on the cold linoleum floor

before she drove me back

the bus was plowed out,
everyone boarded
then we continued
on to the next stop-
also somewhere in barren corn
and pig country-
deservedly called

back then everyone smoked
cigarettes,
so i rolled a joint
to help pass the time

## Cheyenne Wyoming

the scenery after a while
became repetitive;
farm after farm
field after field
crop after crop
they all seem to blend together
until we reached Cheyenne,
with its snow-covered
Laramie mountain range

the bus stopped at the terminal
for a few hours respite,
a new relief driver
needed to be brought in
before we continued

with some time to kill
i walked around a bit,
waving hello to two girls
who are driving by the bus terminal;
that's how i ended up in Laramie

it's a laidback town
where i joined a commune
of college dropouts
who were running
a small, underground newspaper;
i decided to help out

i wrote a column for them
on whatever crossed my young mind-
they paid me with food,
a bed in the back,
plus a young brunette writer

from Connecticut
who also just arrived-
we kept each other warm
at night in the blistering cold,
rugged
wyoming winter nights

this girl was into psychedelic drugs,
it made for some exciting
nights in bed

she was, according to her,
able to see moonbeams
shinning
in the evening sky,
as they came through
the iced-over windows
becoming a kaleidoscope of colors-
it seemed to stimulate her sexual desires;
i was in no rush to leave Laramie

she wrote liberal political essays
which were lost on the local populace.
the paper had some circulation
except only the young folks like us read it,
plus the business owners who advertised
thinking people actually bought the paper

on the side, i wrote copy
for a legitimate newspaper in Cheyenne
to make a few extra dollars

i stayed there till Spring

the state is beautiful,
cowboy boots,

cowboy hats,
wild west attitude;
with great steaks
when i could afford them-
or if i was some older lady's boy toy
for the evening,
like in Manhattan,
which did occur
every now and then

the winters are harsh

often a bunch of us
would go walking
in the woods with snowshoes
searching for wildlife to photograph.
when we inserted the local pictures
in the paper
it always brought us
increased circulation

we also camped out in the woods-
when i would wake in the morning
there is nothing like a western sunrise
in the clean
cool
mountain air to feel alive,
it also helps
if you smoked a joint

the city streets out west are wide
unlike New York,
they have plenty of space

with a lot of spare time
i wrote more poems and songs,

performing them in the evening
at a few bars in town

one day i decided to hitch
a ride back
to the bus terminal in Cheyenne
when i had enough
of western life

the young brunette writer
thought she was pregnant
by one of the many guys
she slept with

i didn't care to wait around
to find out who the father is
since she had a crush on the editor;
she was sleeping with him
every night for months

## Salt Lake City

Salt Lake City is the next terminal
where the bus stopped
for refueling.
nothing else seemed to be happening
until someone on the bus mentioned
the people here are Mormons
and some have more than one wife

i found the fact somewhat interesting

as a young man
i could not understand
why men would marry
so many women
at one time-
when you could quickly hook up
with as many as you want?

the driver told us
as we walked off the bus
the department store next to the terminal
sold Mormon magic underwear,
if we are interested

no shit, magic underwear.
i couldn't believe it-
so i went to look;
they're just long johns-
it blew my mind

my initial feeling of the city
is boring,
very boring,
and very, very white

## San Francisco

it was about six in the evening
when the bus pulled into the terminal.
there were no cell phones back then
i found a pay phone
then dialed the number
Leslie left for me to call her
if i ever came to visit

there was no answer

on the small scrap of paper
was an address-
i asked a cop
walking past me
how i can get to Sixth Street-
he looked at me,
hesitated,
then told me
to get back on the bus
and go home

one of the men on the bus
i spoke with asked me
if i needed a lift somewhere,
his girlfriend is coming
to pick him up

a few minutes later
this beat up rusty Chevy
stopped at the curb,
he waved to me
to get in the back seat;
they drove me to the address

getting out
i had to step over
a guy strung out on the pavement,
young teen hippie hookers
are on the sidewalk
with bell-bottom pants and tie-dye shirts
competing with the pros
on the other corner;
both looking
for johns to party with them

the address i'm looking
for is down the block.
i walk with my back rigid,
trying to exude confidence,
so no one will attack me
trying to steal my guitar
to pawn it for their next fix

standing in front of the house,
i look up
to see a building
in need of major repairs

there are three bells by the front door
none of which have names under them,
i ring all three and wait

a girl opens the door

i ask if Leslie lives there,
only to find out she left about a month ago
and moved,
the girl thinks,
to somewhere with her boyfriend
to join a commune in the desert-

led by some Haight-Asbury guru.
a year or two later
she is in all the newspapers
for aiding in the killing
of wealthy movie stars
in Beverly Hills;
what a waste of a life

with nowhere to hang
i asked the girl
if she knew a place
where i could to sleep for the night
*if you don't mind staying with two lesbians*
*you can sleep here for the evening.*
*my girlfriend is a bartender*
*and will be back when the bar closes,*
*about two this morning*

San Francisco is chilly at night
so i took up her offer,
settled in
on their stained,
ripped sofa
as i looked for bugs
to come crawling out,
but none did;
the girls were personally clean -
but go dumpster diving for furniture

i was exhausted
but had to stay up talking to her
until her girlfriend came home,
then introduced myself,
shared a blunt with them;
both were cool
with me staying over

i found out the girls are bisexual

Gloria is the bartender
and has more tattoos
all over her body,
even in private places,
than anyone i ever met
at this point in my life.

she is somewhat guarded
but has a good sense of humor.
Iris is more outgoing and trusting;
i guess that's why she let me stay
till Gloria came home and has a good heart

we smoked,
talked a lot about stuff
for a few hours

i found some new friends,
good friends, it would turn out later

next morning i went  looking for a job

**west coast living**

the free newspapers
given out on the corners
have jobs listed,
so i applied
to a few as a writer
for the local papers

since i was young,
also sang,
the Chronicle-Examiner hired me
as the entertainment columnist;
my job
was to go to dive bars,
night clubs,
and concerts
to write about them,
while soliciting ads at the same time

the bar owners
always gave me free drinks
to ensure a positive review

this is how i developed a taste for liquor

the first club
i was assigned to assess
was one of the original topless bars in the country,
watch their undressed review
on a makeshift stage-
located in a basement theater
with a low metal ceiling
where the almost naked waitresses
had to bend over people
sitting on the ends

to pass drinks down,
because the aisles are so narrow;
truthfully,
i didn't find it exciting-
too many breasts hanging out,
i felt satiated

my next assignment
was a blues singer
in the Mission District
at another downstairs club
where a local girl,
Sunshine Smyth
was reportedly making waves
with her voice

the day i intended to do the review
i stayed late at the office
writing up a column
on the hippie scene in the city,
until the cleaning crew
came around
and security
told me to go home

i skipped dinner
planning to grab a bite
at the club-
a burger and beer
was my standard meal then;
my stomach could digest
almost anything
in those years

the music started
about ten at night

for the late show

the booze started  to sell
with bare-breasted women
carrying full trays
to the seated customers
while i took a seat
at the far end of the bar,
with an ice cold beer, on tap,
to go with my burger

the singer
was a young local girl
from Sonoma County
with a soulful sound,
giving meaning to every word
in the song;
the place went crazy
when she finished

the manager must have told her
i was there to do a review;
after her set, she came over,
sat at the bar next to me
placing her hand on my lap,
smiling,
when she asked me
how i liked the show

we left the city after a short while
.
Sunshine drove to Marin County
to the Marshall Tavern
where we heard Neil Young sing;
we hit it off-
after a few drinks

she invited me back
to her place
where i stayed
for the rest of the night

the next day i was at work by noon-
since i went out on business
the night before i could come in late-
needless to say
my review was very positive;
i ended up moving in with her

this arrangement lasted
for almost a year
until a sharp talking
talent manager
read my reviews,
came to see her,
offering to take her on tour
with a local band called The Warlocks
(later known as the Grateful Dead)

Sunshine packed her bags,
said goodbye in a letter
left on the kitchen table
while i was at work-
then went on tour
moving in
with her new manager

with nowhere to hang
i called Iris and Gloria
asking if they had space
for me to stay with them again-
they did

it was only for a short time.
i was soon asked
by a record label
to go on tour
with a new rock band,
keep a journal
of their events
for a new album cover
as they traveled
up and down the west coast;
promoting their newly released  songs
in sold out concerts

i took pictures,
hung out with the girls
who flocked to the tour bus and hotels,
while having a hell of a time
taking notes
to review at a later date

## Mexico

the tour ended in San Diego,
with a few bucks in my pocket.
i decided to take a few days off
so i traveled to Baja California

Tijuana is the first city i visited,
it was there i met Catalina
in the hotel's busy bar
where i was staying;
knowing she probably
spotted me as a tourist,
but i didn't care;
she was voluptuous
in a form-fitting red dress
with flowing long auburn hair
and full pink lips

after a few drinks
she said goodbye,
left her phone number on a napkin,
told me to call her tomorrow
then walked out of the hotel

i didn't realize it then-
she played me big time
so i would want
what i couldn't have-
smart on her part

next day we met again.
she suggested
we go together to La Paz
for a few days
to get acquainted

beach, sun, sex, and liquor
were the perfect combination
for me to settle in there
then start to write,
and begin my first novel

a few days
extended to a few weeks,
to a few months,
then two years
while i continued to write
about the rock tour
i was on in California
plus another new book

living was easy
costs were low,
Catalina worked
at the local hotel-
i never asked
what she did;
sometimes,
better not to know

toward the end
of the second year
my novel was finished.

Iris, back in San Francisco,
started to work at a literary agency
since i left.
she became an agent-
and represented me.
my novel was accepted
by a large publisher;
the advance was substantial

la Buena Vida,
the good life

one morning Catalina
turned to me,
looking directly in my face,
and told me she is pregnant

stunned,
i didn't know what to say.
putting her arms
around my neck
she drew me close,
kissed me;
a week later
we married

now, i had to find
a larger place to live;
so we moved inland
where homes
are more affordable

**domestication**

after my daughter was born
we settled into a daily routine.
i'd write in the morning
while she fed the baby,
in the afternoon
we all went to the beach

the royalties
from my book were substantial.
Iris said the publisher
wanted a second book;
plus needed me to go on tour
on the east coast
pushing my novel,
making a bigger name for myself
while also prepping
my soon to be written
second novel

i was hesitant
to go on tour again.
the west coast tour
with the bands was a lot of fun,
but i didn't want to leave Catalina
or my daughter-
touring wears you down

after waiting a month to answer
Iris finally called
said i have no choice,
i had to go.
Catalina was in favor of it,
she never visited the United States
so, one night in bed with her, i said yes

**the east coast tour**

with our passports in hand
we flew to Chicago to start
the east coast tour.

i had a few book signings set up
plus a speaking event
at a music convention

it was there i met a music agent
who years ago
heard me sing in a club
in New York;
he remembered me

Dylan appeared at a venue
in the area
so i was booked to open for him
for one night only

my set was met with standing applause;
it set my life on a new course

the agent agreed to book me
into clubs
in the cities
where the book tour took me

now i was speaking and signing
at book stores and conventions
from Chicago to Maine
then south to Washington D.C.
mostly during the day,
then singing in the evenings-

playing all over the east coast
took most of six months
while Catalina and the baby
lived out of a suitcase
in hotels and motels

New York City was to be our final stop

Catalina was mesmerized by the city.
the publisher arranged
for her to be taken on a tour
while Iris and i were in meetings

later in the evening
after dinner
my wife decided
she wanted to stay in New York,
so we needed both her and the baby
to become citizens-
i found out
my daughter is a citizen
due to my citizenship;
but Catalina had to apply

we found an apartment
over a furniture store in Brooklyn,
and settled in.
my wife applied for a position
in a Spanish hotel in Manhattan;
she told me a start date -
it was as an evening manager
in the bar-
the same type of job
she held in Mexico;
the money was good,
most of it was tips in cash

**the last trip**

the years flew by;
my daughter was almost a teenager.
Catalina was settled in
working nights-
occasionally traveling
back and forth to Mexico
with her American passport
visiting relatives in Tijuana

on her last trip to Mexico
she left my daughter with me
while visiting her mother
when the call came
early one morning

the local police arrested her
for smuggling;
the Policia Federal Ministerial
agency was involved too;
something about money laundering
for a drug cartel

the PFM agent said
Catalina is the mistress
of a big-time cartel chief
who ordered her
to marry an American
so she could travel
between countries
working for the cartel

the agent told me
she would bring jewels
into the states,

sell them,
then deposit the cash
in a shell business account
the cartel set up in New York,
where funds could be wired
back to Mexico

i was heartbroken;
i felt used,
dirty,
deceived,
and depressed

when i was on the phone
with the Mexican agent
i asked if i could speak to her;
she didn't want to talk to me

a few times i tried contacting her
with no success-

finally, a PFM agent told me
she disappeared
while waiting
for a court appearance;
a month later
they found her body
on the side of a road in Tijuana

**family**

at least i had my daughter,
or so i believed-
i loved her,
we had a close relationship
as a father and daughter should have

when she was fifteen
in high school
they were teaching biology
and genetics,
we both did a DNA test-
the results showed
we were not related;
someone else
was her biological father

i never told her-
i couldn't bring myself to tell
the little girl
i loved with all my heart

she lived with me as my daughter,
then went off to college
where she met a young man-
they married,
moved to Chicago
where he is from,
then started to raise a family

every week she would call me-
i miss her terribly

i didn't want to upset her life
or be a drag

so i stayed here
relocating upstate
in the northern woods

to be alone and write

**the call**

O'Bryan sat
listening to me
tell him my life story
until a few people
walked in the bar
looking for the lunch specials

my phone rang-
Vanessa is being discharged
in the late afternoon-
she needs a ride
back to my place;
guess i have a new house guest

driving to the hospital
to pick her up
i stop short
when two suicidal deer
run out of the woods
in front of my car

amazingly i didn't hit them
considering the amount of scotch
i drank all morning-
O'Bryan poured coffee
into me to sober me up-

up here the only thing
i would hit anyway
would be a deer or a tree;
my car made it to the hospital
with no mishaps

**going home**

a nurse wheeled her out
through the double glass doors
to my waiting car;
i helped her sit in the front;
she was thin,
her face was drawn,
pale,
sickly looking,
her clothes hung on her,
too big, not fitting right

we talked on the way back

she apologized to me-
tears flowing down her cheeks,
wanting to stay with me
while she cleaned herself up
staying away from drugs
in the middle of nowhere

i don't know
if she was stroking my ego,
she said she wanted
to be with me

she felt secure,
safe,
appreciated
my kindness

to be truthful
i kind of felt good,
young again
with her around;

it gets lonely
up here in the woods-
plus Vanessa
is my daughter's name

how could i turn my back on her now?

# the end

**other poetry books by the author**

*Scrambled Poems from my Heart*

*A Boutique Bouquet of Poetry and Stories*

*Rumblings of an Old Man*

*Surf Avenue Girl - a semi episodic book*

*Flash Pan Poetry*

*Aliyah - a poetic memoir*

# www.CraetiveFiction.net

www.ingramcontent.com/pod-product-compliance
Lightning Source LLC
Chambersburg PA
CBHW051717040426
**42446CB00008B/937**